I0448163

June 2013

U.S. POSTAL SERVICE

Opportunities to Increase Revenue Exist with Competitive Products; Reviewing Long-Term Results Could Better Inform Promotions Decisions

GAO-13-578

June 2013

GAO Highlights

Highlights of GAO-13-578, a report to congressional requesters

U.S. POSTAL SERVICE

Opportunities to Increase Revenue Exist with Competitive Products; Reviewing Long-Term Results Could Better Inform Promotions Decisions

Why GAO Did This Study

For several years USPS has not generated sufficient revenues to cover its expenses. Although much focus has been on USPS's costs as a way to close the gap between its revenues and expenses, generating additional revenue is also needed. To increase mail volume and revenue, USPS has implemented NSAs, sales, and promotions with a variety of products.

As requested, GAO reviewed (1) the trends and reported results of USPS's sales, promotions, and NSAs, as well as (2) any opportunities and challenges related to generating additional revenue from them. GAO reviewed USPS documents, PRC decisions, and annual reports, and interviewed officials from USPS and PRC. GAO also interviewed mailers, which were selected in part based on participation in NSAs, sales, and promotions. Their views cannot be generalized to all mailers.

What GAO Recommends

GAO recommends that when filing for approval, USPS provide information to PRC about USPS's data collection and analysis plans for estimating the long-term financial results of promotions. GAO also recommends that PRC evaluate USPS's data collection and analysis plans for promotions as part of its review. In commenting on the report, USPS disagreed with the first recommendation, and PRC agreed with both recommendations. USPS stated it does not believe the recommendation will significantly affect the PRC's review process or improve the quality of USPS's business decisions. GAO continues to believe this recommendation has merit, as discussed in this report.

View GAO-13-578. For more information, contact Lorelei St. James at (202) 512-2834 or stjamesl@gao.gov.

What GAO Found

The U.S. Postal Service (USPS) has developed numerous negotiated service agreements (NSA), sales, and promotions since the enactment of the Postal Accountability and Enhancement Act (PAEA) in 2006, and they generate a small but growing portion of USPS total revenue. PAEA established two categories of products: "market dominant," where USPS has a monopoly, and "competitive," which includes all other products, such as shipping services. NSAs, sales, and promotions are generally designed to encourage additional mail volume and revenue through temporary discounts on specific mail products. For example, USPS has offered promotions to incentivize mailers to invest in technology that may increase the value of mail for those mailers over the long-term. No NSAs, sales, or promotions followed the enactment of PAEA until regulations were issued in late 2007. The number of NSAs, sales, and promotions has increased most years since. The revenue generated from NSAs, sales, and promotions has also increased overall. The most revenue was generated by competitive NSAs. Financial results of competitive NSAs are not reported publicly. According to the Postal Regulatory Commission (PRC), which exercises regulatory oversight over USPS, nearly all competitive NSAs have covered their costs. Market dominant NSAs generated little revenue, in part because few were done. Sales and promotions have also generated little revenue.

Opportunities for increasing revenue from NSAs, sales, and promotions are primarily with competitive NSAs, though challenges may limit revenue, and it will likely not offset declines from other products. Continued growth in e-commerce is creating opportunities to generate additional revenue through competitive NSAs. Opportunities to generate additional revenue through market dominant NSAs are limited by low demand for those products. Also, it is difficult for USPS to determine whether any volume and revenue increases directly result from market dominant NSAs because it is difficult to accurately estimate mailers' future mail volume. In addition, USPS and some mailers we spoke with noted that the process for developing both market-dominant and competitive NSAs can be burdensome, hindering the development of new agreements. USPS has taken actions, though, to streamline the process for developing competitive NSAs. Opportunities for generating revenue from sales and promotions are also limited by low demand as well as limited review of the long-term financial results before implementation. USPS has noted that promotions satisfy rate requirements by, for example, helping to generate revenues for USPS. In particular, promotions are used to encourage mail volume over the long term. However, USPS does not provide data and analysis about the potential long-term financial results when submitting promotions to PRC for its approval. As a result, PRC does not assess the methodologies for evaluating the long-term financial results of promotions before implementation. Given USPS's financial situation, USPS should demonstrate how promotions may achieve positive long-term financial results, in order to help maximize the revenue generated by those postage rate discounts.

Contents

Figures

Abbreviations

NSA	negotiated service agreement
OIG	Office of Inspector General
PAEA	Postal Accountability and Enhancement Act
PRC	Postal Regulatory Commission
QR	Quick Response
UPU	Universal Postal Union
USPS	United States Postal Service

June 25, 2013

The Honorable Thomas R. Carper
Chairman
The Honorable Tom Coburn, M.D.
Ranking Member
Committee on Homeland Security and Governmental Affairs
United States Senate

The Honorable Susan M. Collins
The Honorable Carl Levin
United States Senate

For several years, the United States Postal Service (USPS) has not generated sufficient revenues to cover its expenses, putting its mission to provide prompt, reliable, and efficient service at risk. Although much of the focus has been on USPS's costs as the way to close the gap between its revenues and expenses, generating additional revenue is also necessary. As customers increasingly turn to digital communications and online payment methods, total mail volume has decreased precipitously, falling 25 percent from its peak in fiscal year 2006 to fiscal year 2012. As a result, USPS's revenue has declined substantially. In 2012, USPS reached its $15-billion borrowing limit and incurred a $15.9-billion net loss.[1] USPS expects that its expenses will exceed revenue and that mail volume will continue to decline each year through fiscal year 2020.

Among USPS's activities to enhance its revenue are negotiated service agreements (NSA), sales, and promotions designed to increase or sustain mail volume and revenue through temporary discounts on specific mail products. In 2010, we reported on various options to generate additional revenue, including the use of NSAs, as part of a broader report

---

[1] The $15.9-billion net loss includes $11.1 billion for two required payments to prefund future retiree health benefits. Originally due at the end of fiscal year 2011, USPS's $5.5 billion retiree health benefit payment was delayed until August 1, 2012. Pub. L. No. 112-74, § 632, 125 Stat. 786, 928 (Dec. 23, 2011). USPS missed that payment as well as the $5.6-billion payment that was due on September 30, 2012. Even though USPS did not make these payments, it recorded a loss for the obligation to make these payments.

GAO-13-578 USPS Revenue Options

on options to facilitate USPS's progress toward financial sustainability.[2] Since that time, USPS has developed dozens more NSAs, sales, and promotions, which you asked us to review. We examined (1) the NSAs, sales, and promotions USPS has developed and their reported financial results, and (2) any opportunities to generate additional revenue from NSAs, sales, and promotions and any challenges that could hinder their development and implementation.

To describe the NSAs, sales, and promotions that USPS has developed, as well as their reported financial results, we reviewed public and non-public documents. To summarize the financial results of NSAs, we examined non-public versions of USPS's Cost and Revenue Analysis reports as well as other non-public USPS documents that included the volume, cost, and revenue of individual NSAs. We also reviewed USPS data collection reports for market dominant NSAs. To summarize the number of, and results from, USPS sales and promotions, we reviewed USPS documents requesting approval for sales and promotions and obtained additional data from USPS on the estimated results of sales and promotions. We assessed the reliability of these data sources by interviewing USPS officials, and determined that the data were sufficiently reliable for our reporting purposes. We also reviewed the Postal Regulatory Commission (PRC) conclusions about NSAs, sales, and promotions in their *Annual Compliance Determination Reports*.[3]

To identify and assess any opportunities to generate additional revenue from NSAs, sales, and promotions, as well as challenges, if any, that could hinder their development and implementation, we reviewed USPS and PRC documents, and conducted interviews with stakeholders. Specifically, we reviewed relevant regulations, PRC proceedings, and internal USPS evaluations of NSAs. We also conducted interviews with officials from USPS, PRC, and 15 "mailers" to enhance our understanding of the circumstances in which NSAs, sales, and promotions are developed and implemented.[4] We selected mailers that both have and

---

[2] GAO, *U.S. Postal Service: Strategies and Options to Facilitate Progress toward Financial Viability*, GAO-10-455 (Washington, D.C.: Apr. 12, 2010).

[3] The PRC's *Annual Compliance Determination Report* is an after-the-fact review of the performance of USPS, focusing primarily on financial transparency and compliance with pricing and service performance standards.

[4] We defined a "mailer" as an entity that prepares and/or presents mailings to USPS.

have not participated in NSAs, sales, and promotions, as well as other factors. We also spoke with industry associations that represent major USPS mailers. The views of mailers and industry associations cannot be generalized to all mailers and industry associations because the sampled mailers were selected as part of a nonprobability sample. Appendix I contains a detailed discussion of our scope and methodology.

We conducted this performance audit from September 2012 to June 2013 in accordance with generally accepted government auditing standards. Those standards require that we plan and perform the audit to obtain sufficient, appropriate evidence to provide a reasonable basis for our findings and conclusions based on our audit objectives. We believe that the evidence obtained provides a reasonable basis for our findings and conclusions based on our audit objectives.

Background

An NSA is a customized contract between USPS and a specific entity—often a mailer or foreign postal operator—typically lasting a year or more. NSAs provide customer-specific rates—generally lower prices on specific mail products—in exchange for meeting volume targets and mail preparation requirements. The goal of these agreements is generally to encourage additional mail volume and revenue. For example, an NSA may provide a postage rate discount, paid to the mailer as a rebate at the end of a fiscal year, for all mail volume above a specific threshold.

The Postal Accountability and Enhancement Act (PAEA)[5] authorized USPS to create NSAs for two discrete categories of mail products, market dominant and competitive, as outlined in table 1.[6] The market dominant category includes products for which USPS has a monopoly or would be

---

[5] Pub. L. No. 109-435, 120 Stat. 3198 (Dec. 20, 2006).

[6] USPS had the ability to create NSAs prior to enactment of PAEA. In 2002, PRC determined NSAs were legally permissible under the Postal Reorganization Act of 1970 (PRA) because it gave USPS "a clear mandate to innovate by developing effective and efficient services adapted to the needs of the Nation's mail users." See PRC, *Report to the Congress: Authority of the United States Postal Service to Introduce New Products and Services and to Enter Into Rate and Service Agreements with Individual Customers or Groups of Customers* (Feb. 11, 2002). According to PRC in 2011, "there was a consensus among stakeholders that the standard regulatory process used to evaluate NSAs under the PRA was unnecessarily complex and time consuming." See PRC, *Section 701 Report* (Sept. 22, 2011).

able to exercise substantial market power, such as First-Class Mail and Standard Mail. Competitive products are all other types of mail, and include primarily shipping services such as Priority Mail, Express Mail, and Parcel Select.

The legal requirements for NSAs differ based on whether the postal products are market dominant or competitive. PAEA requires market dominant NSAs to improve the net financial position or enhance the performance of operational functions of USPS so long as the agreement does not cause unreasonable harm to the marketplace. Also, market dominant product NSAs must be made available to "similarly situated mailers."[7] PAEA requires competitive NSAs, as well as competitive products in general, to cover their attributable costs, meaning they must generate more revenue than the costs attributable to delivery of the products, such as the labor involved in handling that mail.[8] Further, competitive products overall, including NSAs, must contribute at least 5.5 percent of USPS's institutional costs—that is, overhead costs not directly related to the delivery of products.

As directed by PAEA, PRC issued final regulations in 2007 that established procedures for its reviews of competitive and market dominant NSAs, as summarized in table 1.[9] As with all postal rate changes, USPS must obtain approval from PRC prior to implementing NSAs. PRC has approved all NSAs proposed by USPS through fiscal year 2012. PRC also reviews NSAs after implementation for compliance with regulatory criteria, in its *Annual Compliance Determination Report*.

---

[7] Pub. L. No. 109-435, § 201, codified at 39 U.S.C. 3622(c)(10).

[8] Pub. L. No. 109-435, § 201, codified at 39 U.S.C. 3633(a)(2).

[9] PRC, *Order Establishing Ratemaking Regulations for Market Dominant and Competitive Products*, Order No. 43, Docket No. RM2007-1, October 29, 2007.

Table 1: Requirements for Negotiated Service Agreements (NSA)

Mail products		Requirements
Competitive		• For each competitive product, NSA must recover its attributable costs.
Express Mail	Fastest expedited delivery	
First-Class Packages[a]	Packages less than 16 ounces	• Competitive products, collectively, including NSAs, must contribute at least 5.5 percent of USPS's total institutional costs.[b]
Priority Mail	First-Class Mail more than 13 ounces and any other mail matter less than 13 ounces with expedited delivery	
Parcel Select	Ground delivery service for large and medium sized shippers	
Parcel Return Service	Return service for large and medium sized shippers	
International	All international competitive products	
Market dominant		• NSAs must either:
First-Class Mail	Cards, letters, "flats"[c]	o Improve the net financial position of USPS, or
Standard Mail	Advertising, circulars, catalogs, some small parcels	o Enhance operational functions.
Periodicals	Magazines, newsletters	• NSAs may not cause unreasonable harm to the marketplace.
Package Services	Merchandise, printed material	
International	All international market dominant products	• NSAs must be available to similarly situated mailers.

Source: GAO summary of statute and Postal Regulatory Commission (PRC) regulations.

[a]The First-Class Package Services product was moved from the market dominant to the competitive category in fiscal year 2012.

[b]USPS and PRC calculate total institutional costs for each fiscal year. All competitive products must generate revenue above costs attributable to the delivery of those competitive products at least as much as 5.5 percent of total institutional costs.

[c]"Flats" are defined as mail pieces that exceed the dimensions of a normal letter but remain flat, such as large envelopes, newsletters, and magazines.

To increase or sustain mail volume and revenue, USPS has also provided short-term discounts, called sales or promotions, on specific mail products for groups of mailers, in contrast to NSAs, which are agreements with individual mailers for longer periods. Sales—often called price incentive programs—have sought to increase, or curb the decline of, mail volume by temporarily offering a discount (paid through a rebate) to mailers whose mail volume exceeds a predetermined volume threshold during a specific period. Some sales were offered in the summer, when USPS stated it had excess capacity in its system. These sales were designed to generate revenue during the sale period and not necessarily to have long-term benefits. After 2010, USPS began offering promotions instead of sales, which also provide temporary discounts, but seek to increase the long-term value of mail by, for example, integrating mobile technology into mailers' advertising campaigns. As with all postal rate changes, USPS must obtain approval from PRC prior to implementing sales and promotions.[10] PRC reviews whether the proposed sales and promotions meet postal rate regulations that include several qualifying factors such as whether sales and promotions help assure adequate revenues for USPS. See appendix II for a full list of these objectives and factors of postal rate regulation.

Since 2007, USPS Has Developed Numerous NSAs, Sales, and Promotions That Have Generated a Small but Growing Portion of USPS's Total Revenue

Number and Revenue Have Increased since 2007

The number of NSAs, sales, and promotions has increased in most years since the enactment of PAEA. There were no new NSAs approved following the enactment of PAEA until PRC regulations governing NSAs were issued in October 2007. As seen in table 2, the majority of NSAs have been with competitive products. Starting in fiscal year 2011, USPS began using "umbrella" products that allow multiple mailers to agree to similar NSAs. As a result, the total number of NSA-product requests for approval in the table below appears to decline in 2011 and 2012, when in fact the total number of individual contracts with mailers has continued to grow.[11]

---

[10] Market dominant products are subject to a price cap for each class of mail equal to the annual Consumer Price Index—All Urban Consumers.

[11] Table 2 includes NSA requests approved by PRC since the enactment of PAEA, rather than active NSAs, for two reasons. First, many NSAs are active across multiple fiscal years, so reporting active NSAs can produce misleading totals. Second, there were active NSAs in fiscal years 2007 and 2008 that were approved before the implementation of new regulations in October 2007, and are thus not directly comparable to later NSAs approved under PAEA regulations.

Table 2: Negotiated Service Agreement (NSA) Requests Approved by PRC since the Enactment of PAEA, by Fiscal Year

Mail type	2007	2008	2009	2010	2011	2012
Competitive						
Domestic[a]	0	1	32	13	14	32
International[b]	0	16	34	112	50	23
Total competitive	**0**	**17**	**66**	**125**	**64**	**55**
Market dominant						
Domestic[c]	0	0	0	0	1	1
International[d]	0	0	1	3	3	4
Total market dominant	**0**	**0**	**1**	**3**	**4**	**5**
Total NSA requests approved	**0**	**17**	**67**	**128**	**68**	**60**

Source: PRC.

[a]These figures represent the number of domestic, competitive NSA requests approved by PRC since the enactment of PAEA. One domestic, competitive NSA request was for an "umbrella" product that allows USPS to enter into individual contracts, all with similar terms, without filing the contracts with PRC for pre-implementation review. This product involves Priority Mail and was approved in fiscal year 2011. Overall, domestic, competitive NSAs have been approved for Priority Mail, Express Mail, Parcel Select, Parcel Return Service, and First-Class Package Service mail products. Some agreements utilize multiple mail products.

[b]As with domestic, competitive NSAs, these figures represent the number of NSA requests approved by PRC since the enactment of PAEA. Three international, competitive NSA requests were for "umbrella" products that allow USPS to enter into individual contracts, all with similar terms, which are filed at the PRC, but not for pre-implementation review.

[c]These figures represent the number of domestic, market dominant NSA requests approved by PRC since the enactment of PAEA. These figures do not include three NSAs that were filed after enactment of PAEA in December 2006, but before PRC updated its regulations governing NSAs in October 2007.

[d]As with domestic NSAs, these figures represent the number of NSA requests approved by PRC since the enactment of PAEA. Most international, market dominant NSAs are with foreign postal operators.

The first sales were offered in fiscal year 2009, in part as a response to the decline in mail volume resulting from the recession, and USPS has since offered a variety of promotions (see table 3 below).

Table 3: Number of Sales and Promotions Approved by PRC, by Fiscal Year

Sales and promotions	2009	2010	2011	2012
Sales	3	1	2	0
Promotions	0	0	1	1
Total	**3**	**1**	**3**	**1**

Source: GAO analysis of USPS documents.

GAO-13-578 USPS Revenue Options

USPS data show that revenue generated from NSAs, sales, and promotions has generally increased each year since the enactment of PAEA, with most of the revenue generated by competitive product NSAs. We cannot report the specific revenue generated by competitive NSAs because of the proprietary nature of data related to competitive products. However, the total revenue generated as part of all NSAs increased over 240 percent from fiscal year 2009 to 2012, though it remains a small portion of USPS's total revenue (see fig. 1). Market dominant NSAs generated a relatively small portion of this revenue, partly because there have been few such agreements. Beyond NSAs, sales and promotions have also generated limited revenue since the first sale in 2009. As discussed below, it is not clear how much net revenue USPS has generated from market dominant NSAs or sales and promotions.[12]

---

[12] For the purposes of this report, "net revenue" refers to the revenue, minus attributable costs and discounts, above what would have been earned by USPS in the absence of the NSA, sale, or promotion (called "net contribution" by USPS).

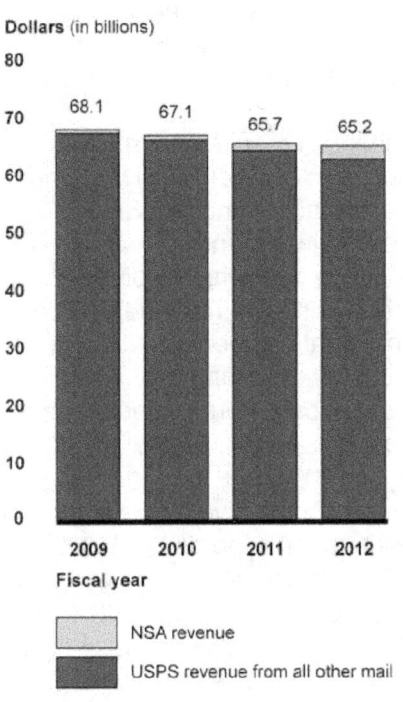

Figure 1: USPS Revenue from Negotiated Service Agreements (NSA) and Other Mail, Fiscal Years 2009 to 2012

Dollars (in billions)

2009: 68.1
2010: 67.1
2011: 65.7
2012: 65.2

Fiscal year

- NSA revenue
- USPS revenue from all other mail

Source: USPS.

USPS Has Developed Numerous Competitive Product NSAs; Most Have Covered Costs and Generated a Small but Growing Portion of Total USPS Revenue

"Competitive" products are those for which USPS does not have a monopoly or is not able to exercise substantial market power. These products primarily include shipping services such as Priority Mail, Express Mail, Parcel Select, and Parcel Return.

Source: GAO summary based on USPS information.

Since the enactment of PAEA, the number of competitive NSAs has grown substantially. PRC has approved 327 domestic and international competitive NSA product requests through fiscal year 2012. A number of these NSA requests are actually "umbrella" products that include numerous individual contracts, all with similar terms. Counting these individual contracts separately illustrates the substantial number of NSAs, with 446 domestic and international competitive NSAs active in fiscal year 2012 alone.

According to USPS officials and a mailer we spoke with, the increased number of competitive NSAs was due mainly to increased experience with NSA contracts and product enhancements. For example, according to these officials, USPS and PRC processes associated with developing competitive NSAs have become more efficient as a result of improved costing techniques and additional experience developing contracts with mailers. USPS and PRC also worked together to develop umbrella products that allow multiple mailers to agree to similar discounts for related mail products. Product enhancements may have also increased USPS's ability to attract more business with NSAs. For example, officials from USPS and a mailer we spoke with noted that USPS's ability to track packages' transit times and its delivery performance improvements for parcels have made USPS products more attractive to customers.

The financial results of competitive product NSAs are not reported publicly, but according to PRC, most such agreements have covered their costs, and according to USPS, these agreements have generally been successful in enhancing revenue. According to PRC, all domestic competitive NSAs have complied with the legal requirements, including that they generate revenue that covers their attributable costs. Four international competitive NSAs in fiscal year 2012, however, did not cover their costs. According to PRC, the international competitive NSAs that did not cover costs were projected to cover costs when USPS filed its request.[13]

Although competitive NSAs are collectively profitable, these agreements generate a small portion of USPS's total revenue and help cover less of USPS's institutional costs than market dominant products.[14] Competitive products overall, including NSAs, generate a relatively small part of USPS's total revenue because they generally involve much lower mail volumes than market dominant products. Additionally, total revenue from competitive products covers less of USPS's institutional costs than the revenue from the two major market dominant products, First-Class Mail and Standard Mail.

---

[13] In its fiscal year 2012 *Annual Compliance Determination Report*, PRC directed USPS to modify its international competitive NSA cost models for certain international products to accurately develop costs, or to increase its cost contingency factor to accommodate costs that cannot be modeled.

[14] For the purposes of this report, "profit" refers to revenue above attributable costs.

Since Enactment of PAEA, USPS Has Developed Few Market Dominant NSAs and Generated Limited, if Any, Net Revenue from Them

"Market dominant" products are those for which USPS has a monopoly or would be able to exercise substantial market power. These primarily include First-Class Mail, Standard Mail, Periodicals, and some types of Package Services.

Source: GAO summary based on USPS information.

"Net revenue" refers to the revenue, minus attributable costs and discounts, above what would have been earned by USPS in the absence of the NSA, sale, or promotion (called "net contribution" by USPS).

Source: GAO summary based on USPS information.

USPS has implemented few market dominant NSAs. USPS has been granted approval by PRC to implement two domestic, market dominant NSAs since the enactment of PAEA, though only one of these was active, as of May 2013. In fiscal year 2012, there was one active market dominant domestic NSA, and eight active market dominant international NSAs. USPS has implemented few such NSAs in part because of the decline in demand for market dominant mail products, as discussed further below.

Domestic, market dominant NSAs have likely generated limited, if any, net revenue (see fig. 2). Most of these agreements were implemented prior to the enactment of PAEA. According to USPS, all domestic market dominant NSAs have generated net revenue of $68.5 million dollars to date. However, PRC, using a different methodology that is discussed below, estimates a net loss of $11.8 million for all domestic market dominant NSAs.

For example, the USPS and PRC estimates of net revenue for the Discover NSA approved in fiscal year 2011 differ substantially. USPS's estimate of net revenue assumes that all volume greater than the projected volume is because of the rebate. USPS developed its estimates of projected volume based on Discover's mail volume history as well as other qualitative factors. PRC used a quantitative methodology based on product elasticities—that is, the estimated sensitivity of total product mail volume to price changes—associated with the mail product involved. As a result, USPS estimated net revenue of about $24 million in the first year of the NSA with Discover, while PRC estimated USPS lost over $4 million. As discussed further below, PRC has encouraged USPS to identify a more reliable method for evaluating the impact of market dominant NSAs.

Figure 2: Estimated Net Revenue from Domestic, Market-Dominant Negotiated Service Agreements, 2003 to 2014

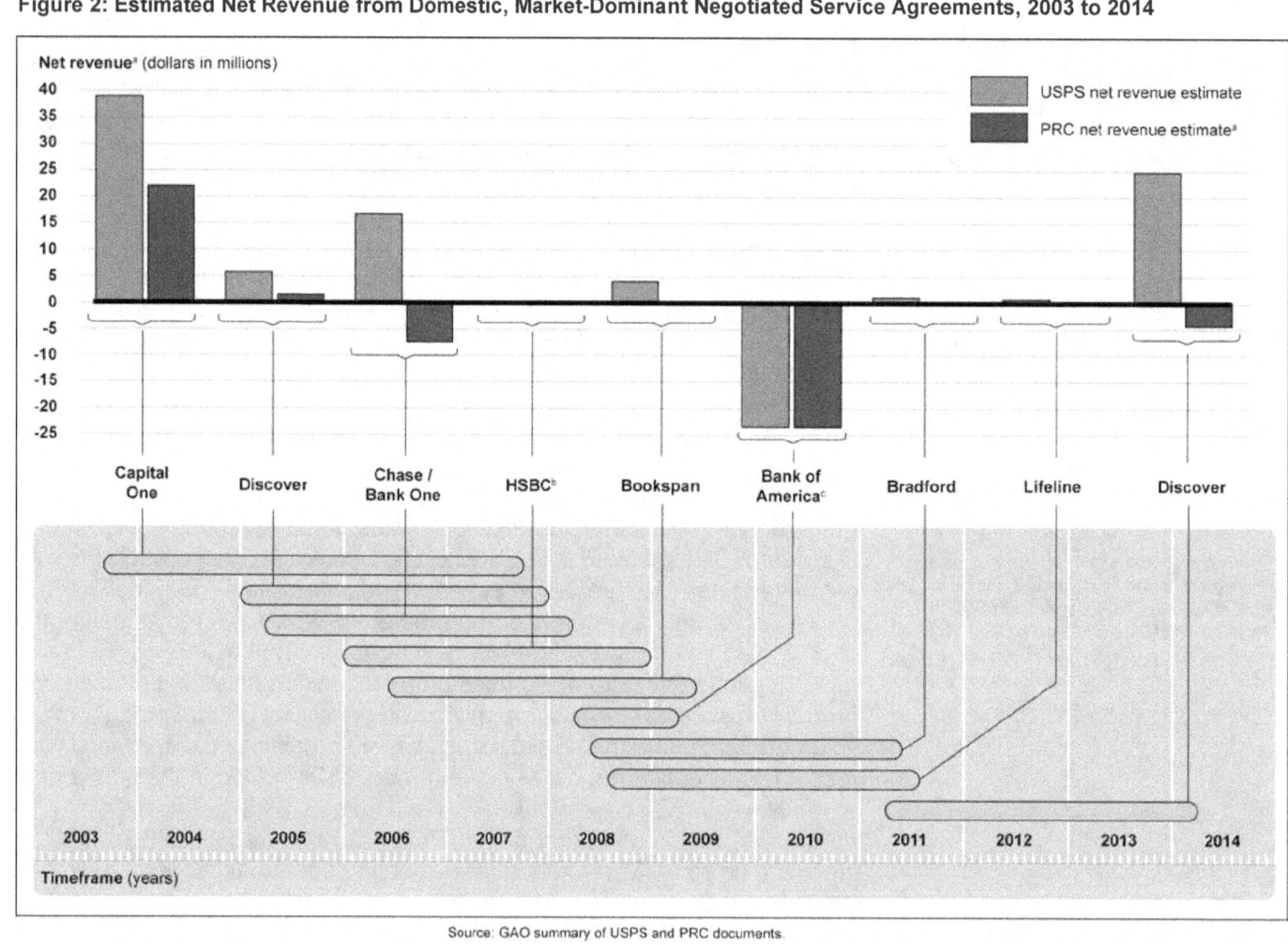

Source: GAO summary of USPS and PRC documents.

[a]USPS and PRC have used different methodologies for estimating the net revenue generated by domestic, market dominant negotiated service agreements. Net revenue refers to the revenue, minus attributable costs and discounts, above what would have been earned by USPS (called "net contribution" by USPS).

[b]No discounts were paid pursuant to the HSBC contract because it did not reach the discount threshold during any of the three contract years.

[c]The Bank of America contract was cancelled after the first year of the contract because of the estimated loss of revenue.

International market dominant NSAs implemented since the enactment of PAEA consist mainly of agreements with foreign posts and are estimated to have lost approximately $25 million in net revenue in fiscal year 2012, according to USPS. However, PRC has noted that the volume sent under the NSAs generated smaller losses than what would have occurred if the volumes were sent under Universal Postal Union (UPU) international postal rates. According to USPS officials, agreements with foreign posts are governed by UPU rates, which are developed based on domestic postal rates. The U.S. has low domestic postal rates compared to other countries, and as a result, its UPU-established inbound mail rates do not allow some international NSAs to cover their costs.[15] As PRC explained in its 2012 *Annual Compliance Determination Report*, the "current UPU formula [for setting international postal rates] adversely affects the financial performance of inbound mail [NSAs]." Similar to competitive domestic NSAs, the first international market dominant NSAs after PAEA were active in fiscal year 2009.[16]

Since Enactment of PAEA, USPS Has Increased Sales and Promotions but Generated Limited, if Any, Net Revenue

USPS has implemented six sales and three promotions, all of which offered temporary discounts to mailers to sustain and grow mail volume. USPS estimates that these sales and promotions have earned a maximum net revenue of about $184 million (see table 4). According to USPS data, some sales and promotions are estimated to have generated little to no net revenue during the program periods. However, according to USPS officials, these incentives have generally been successful in that they will eventually help sustain mail volume. Officials said that mailers who have taken advantage of sales and promotions have increased their overall mail volume, while those who have not participated in these programs have kept their volume steady or reduced it. Further, USPS's long-term goal for promotions is that they will enhance the value of the mail for mailers and therefore help to keep mailers in the mail beyond the program period. It is unclear the extent to which sales and promotions are accomplishing this goal, as discussed below. PRC approves sales and promotions under the requirements for setting rates and has conducted after the fact reviews of two sales. According to PRC officials, they were

---

[15] Some USPS agreements with foreign posts are long-standing agreements that were in place before the enactment of PAEA. Though some of these agreements do not cover costs, the agreements improve the net financial position of USPS by allowing contract-specific rates for above-UPU cost coverage rates where applicable.

[16] International NSAs prior to the enactment of PAEA were classified as International Customized Mail Agreements (ICM) and were not comparable to NSAs after the enactment of PAEA.

unable to evaluate the results of the other sales or promotions because USPS did not provide sufficient data to PRC.

Table 4: Estimated Net Revenue of Sales and Promotions, Fiscal Years 2009 to 2013

Name of sale or promotion	Fiscal year	Product(s)	Duration of program period	USPS estimate of net revenue (during program period)[a]	PRC estimate of net revenue (during program period)[b]
Sales					
Standard Mail Volume Incentive Pricing Program[c]	2009	Standard Mail	4 months	$24.1 million	-36.9 million
Saturation Mail Incentive Program[d]	2009 - 2010	Standard Mail	12 months	$18.9 million	Not estimated
First-Class Mail Incentive Program[e]	2009	First-Class Mail	3 months	$18 million	-$7 million
Standard Mail Volume Incentive Pricing Program[c]	2010	Standard Mail	5 months	$48 to $65 million	Not estimated
Saturation-HD Mail Incentive Program[f]	2011 - 2012	Standard Mail	12 months	$14.5 million	Not estimated
"Reply Rides Free" – First Class Mail Incentive[g]	2011 - 2012	First-Class Mail	12 months	$14.3 million	Not estimated
Promotions[h]					
Mobile barcode promotion[i]	2011	First-Class and Standard Mail	2 months	$13 million	Not estimated
Mobile barcode promotion[i]	2012	First-Class and Standard Mail	2 months	-$5 million to $2 million	Not estimated
Holiday mobile shopping promotion[i]	2013	First-Class and Standard Mail	2 weeks	- $1 million to $14 million	Not estimated

Source: USPS.

[a]Net revenue refers to the revenue, minus attributable costs and discounts, above what would have been earned by USPS in the absence of the sale or promotion (called "net contribution" by USPS).

[b]PRC has not evaluated the results of most sales and promotions because of data limitations.

[c]Offered a 30 percent postage discount on Standard Mail volume above a threshold volume tailored to each mailer.

[d]Offered postage discounts for saturation mail volume above threshold volumes tailored to each mailer.

[e]Offered 20 percent postage discount on presorted First-Class Mail volume above a threshold volume tailored to each mailer.

[f]Offered postage discounts on saturation and high density volume above a threshold volume tailored to each mailer.

[g]Offered postage discount for First-Class Mail automation letters above a threshold volume tailored to each mailer.

[h]USPS has noted that many of these promotions are designed to have an impact on mail volume and revenue beyond the program period by, for example, helping to increase the value of mail for mailers. However, USPS has not reported any estimates of the long-term financial results.

[i]Offered postage discount to First-Class and Standard cards, letters, and flats that included a two-dimensional mobile barcode.

| Sales | USPS offered sales on First-Class Mail and Standard Mail products to encourage additional mail volume and revenue during a historically low-volume period. For example, USPS's first sale was held during 4 months in the summer of 2009, offering a 30 percent discount for Standard Mail on incremental volume above a threshold volume tailored to each participating mailer. USPS stated that it had the ability to offer a steep discount on any mail volume sent above what the customer mailed during the same four month period in the summer of 2009 because it had significant excess capacity and, as a result, there was little incremental cost for USPS to mail the additional volume. USPS conducted a similar sale in the summer of 2010 because of the estimated profits from the first sale, as well as continued excess capacity. |

USPS estimated maximum net revenue of $126 million for the sales it has conducted, though PRC has estimated different results than USPS in every case where PRC has examined the net revenue. Specifically, PRC estimated that the 2009 sales programs—Standard Mail Volume Incentive Pricing Program and First-Class Mail Incentive Program—lost money for USPS during the time in which it offered the discount. PRC estimated a $7 million net loss for the First-Class Mail Incentive Program, and an approximately $37 million net loss for the Standard Mail Volume Incentive Pricing Program. As with domestic, market dominant NSAs, PRC used a different methodology than USPS to estimate the net revenue generated by these sales. The different methodologies used by PRC and USPS to evaluate discount programs for market dominant products are discussed further below. According to PRC, they have not evaluated the results of all sales because of corrupt or missing USPS data.

| Promotions | USPS estimated a maximum net value of about $58 million for promotions conducted to date (see table above). USPS has offered promotions as temporary discounts on First-Class Mail and Standard Mail products to help connect physical mail to technology, which USPS assumed would increase the value of mail for mailers and help sustain mail volume and revenue in the future. For example, USPS promotions encourage retailers to print Quick Response (QR) codes on physical mail pieces, which allow the consumer to scan the QR code with their mobile device, directing them to the retailers' website, as illustrated in figure 3. |

Figure 3: How Mobile Quick Response (QR) Codes Work

| Mailer prints QR code on letter mail. | Consumer scans QR code using mobile device. | Consumer is directed to mailer's mobile website. |

Source: GAO.

USPS has used promotions to increase the value of the mail for mailers so that they sustain their use of mail. Specifically, USPS uses promotions as tools to develop innovative products, such as the use of discounts as incentives for mailers to invest in technology that may increase the value of mail over the long term. For instance, USPS implemented the 2012 holiday mobile shopping promotion for 2 weeks and gave a 2 percent discount to First-Class Mail and Standard Mail cards, letters, and flats that included a QR code.[17] With this promotion, USPS sought to provide incentives for more mailers to use mobile barcodes to direct consumers to their websites for more information on sales. Officials told us that USPS believed direct mail that included such barcodes is more valuable because it makes the mail a multi-media experience. USPS noted that by increasing the value of its mail products it can retain as much advertising revenue as possible. An additional component of this promotion was the potential for customers to earn an additional 1 percent discount if their volume exceeded specified Priority Mail thresholds. Although USPS has estimated the financial result of promotions for the program period, it has not provided any estimates of the long-term financial results to PRC, as discussed in more detail later in this report.

---

[17] Mobile barcodes, called Quick Response "QR" codes, when scanned by a mobile phone, can direct the user to an Internet website.

Opportunities for Increasing Revenue from NSAs, Sales, and Promotions Are Primarily from Competitive NSAs, though Challenges May Limit Revenue

Opportunities Exist to Generate Additional Revenue from Competitive NSAs but Will Likely Not Offset Declines from Other Products

Opportunities Exist Because of Continued Growth in E-Commerce

Opportunities exist to generate additional revenue through competitive product NSAs primarily because of merchandise shipments associated with the continued growth in e-commerce.[18] USPS projects that total shipping and package volume will grow by about 33 percent by the end of fiscal year 2017, after increasing about 7.5 percent in fiscal year 2012. Expansion of e-commerce has been a key factor in the growth of these products, most of which are competitive. Moreover, e-commerce continues to grow and has not reached its full potential because of accessibility, returns, payment, and security concerns. Companies that can solve these shortcomings may garner additional business, and USPS may be able to develop NSAs with these companies.

Other factors may allow USPS to continue taking advantage of the growth in e-commerce and generate additional revenue through competitive product NSAs. First, even if USPS moves to a 5-day delivery schedule, it

---

[18] Electronic commerce, or e-commerce, refers to conducting business (e.g., buying and selling products and services) on the Internet.

has proposed that it would continue to deliver packages on Saturday to maintain its advantage of delivering to every household 6 days a week without a surcharge.[19] Second, although USPS faces private-sector competitors with entrenched market share of the package delivery business, USPS has certain competitive advantages. Although FedEx and UPS lead the high-volume business-to-business package delivery market, it can be very expensive for them to deliver single items to residential addresses, particularly in rural areas. Along with such "last mile" delivery advantages, USPS also has special access to some large residential buildings.

While the growth and opportunities associated with competitive products are substantial, additional growth is not likely to offset declines in other products. Competitive products taken as a whole are a modest piece of USPS's total revenue, and generate relatively low profits, compared to the most profitable market dominant products, First-Class Mail and Standard Mail (see fig. 4).[20] Even with robust growth in competitive products, including NSAs involving those products, it is extremely unlikely that this additional revenue will offset the projected declines in First-Class Mail and other products.

---

[19] Provisions in annual USPS appropriations since 1984 mandate 6-day-a-week delivery and rural mail delivery at certain levels. These provisions have specified that "6-day delivery and rural delivery of mail shall continue at not less than the 1983 level." See e.g., Pub. L. No. 111-117, 123 Stat. 3200 (Dec. 16, 2009).

[20] While these products generated a profit, USPS also had significant institutional costs, which along with required payments to prefund its future retiree health benefits, contributed to a $15.9 billion net loss for USPS in fiscal year 2012.

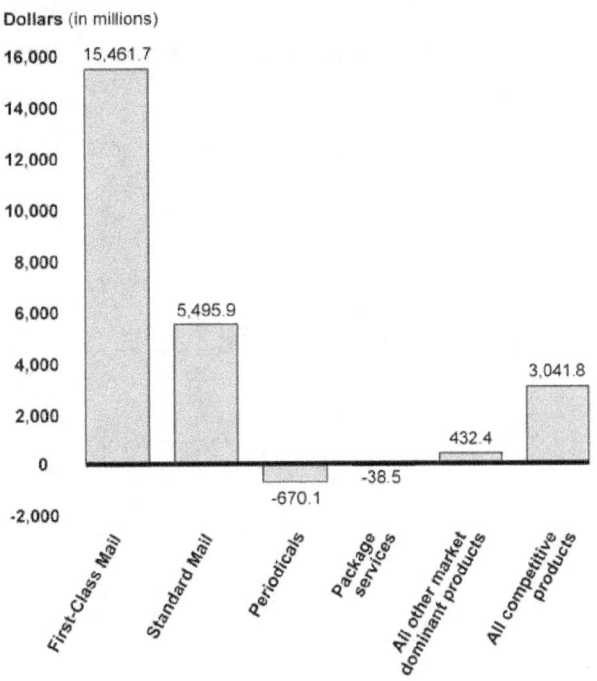

Figure 4: Profit from Market Dominant Products and All Competitive Products, Fiscal Year 2012

Dollars (in millions)

Sources: USPS cost and revenue analysis report, fiscal year 2012.

Note: Profit refers to revenue above attr butable costs, and does not reflect USPS's institutional costs.

Process for Developing Competitive NSAs Could Limit Additional Revenue

USPS's ability to generate additional revenue from competitive product NSAs may also face challenges because of the length of the process to develop NSAs. The USPS Office of Inspector General (OIG) reported in 2011 that, despite improvements, the preparation and review process for new product approvals puts USPS at a competitive disadvantage in terms of speed to market.[21] Three mailers we spoke with that had NSAs with USPS said that the time it took to develop and obtain approval for NSAs was long when compared to negotiating contracts with USPS's competitors, and three other mailers also described the process as lengthy (see fig. 5). Four of the mailers we spoke with that had not

[21] USPS Office of Inspector General, Risk Analysis Research Center, *Postal Service Revenue: Structure, Facts, and Future Possibilities*, RARC-WP-12-002 (Oct. 6, 2011).

developed NSAs with USPS also told us that they perceive the process of developing NSAs as burdensome, which deters them from pursuing such agreements.

Figure 5: Negotiated Service Agreement (NSA) Development Process

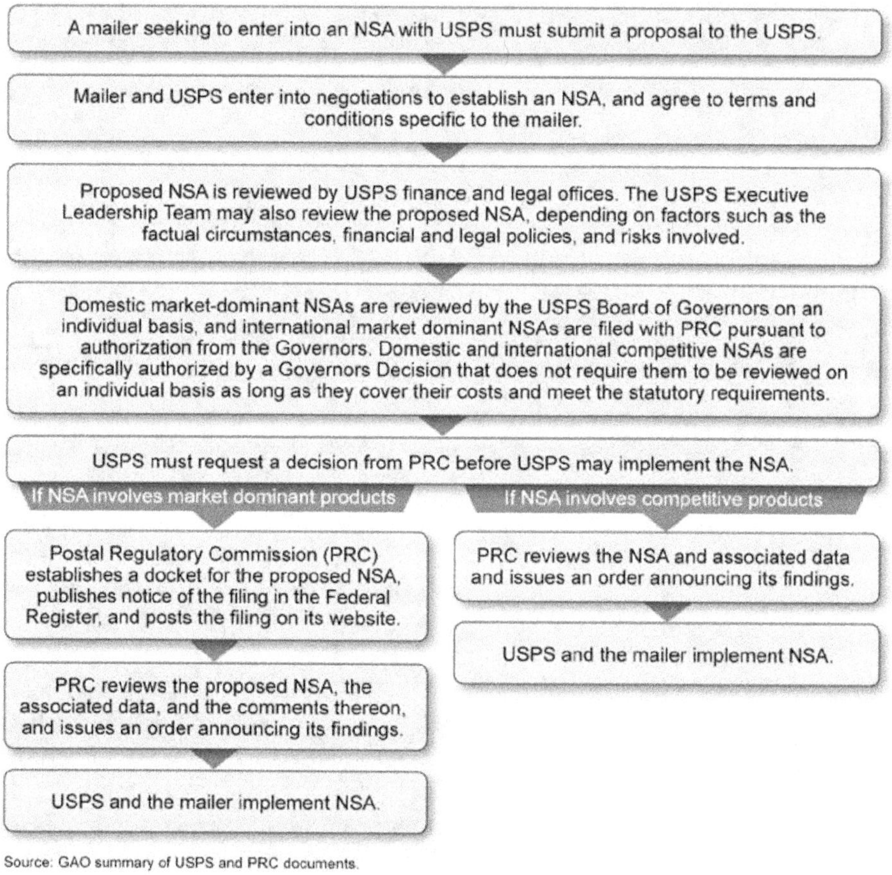

A mailer seeking to enter into an NSA with USPS must submit a proposal to the USPS.

Mailer and USPS enter into negotiations to establish an NSA, and agree to terms and conditions specific to the mailer.

Proposed NSA is reviewed by USPS finance and legal offices. The USPS Executive Leadership Team may also review the proposed NSA, depending on factors such as the factual circumstances, financial and legal policies, and risks involved.

Domestic market-dominant NSAs are reviewed by the USPS Board of Governors on an individual basis, and international market dominant NSAs are filed with PRC pursuant to authorization from the Governors. Domestic and international competitive NSAs are specifically authorized by a Governors Decision that does not require them to be reviewed on an individual basis as long as they cover their costs and meet the statutory requirements.

USPS must request a decision from PRC before USPS may implement the NSA.

If NSA involves market dominant products

Postal Regulatory Commission (PRC) establishes a docket for the proposed NSA, publishes notice of the filing in the Federal Register, and posts the filing on its website.

PRC reviews the proposed NSA, the associated data, and the comments thereon, and issues an order announcing its findings.

USPS and the mailer implement NSA.

If NSA involves competitive products

PRC reviews the NSA and associated data and issues an order announcing its findings.

USPS and the mailer implement NSA.

Source: GAO summary of USPS and PRC documents.

USPS officials said that they employ a "risk-based" process for evaluating proposed NSAs, which involves differing levels of scrutiny depending on the size of the proposed agreement. Specifically, USPS has a multi-step internal process for developing and approving competitive NSAs. First, the agreement is generally negotiated by sales representatives using costing templates, which allows them to develop agreements that are estimated to cover the costs of the particular product involved. USPS's finance office also examines each agreement to ensure that it is projected to cover its costs. USPS conducts a "business evaluation" to ensure that the agreement is likely to generate profit for USPS. USPS's Law Department reviews an agreement throughout its development. USPS officials noted that carrying out business evaluations can be difficult because of the availability of the data and the ability to turn the analysis around quickly. Competitive NSAs are also authorized by the USPS Board of Governors, subject to internal USPS review, as well as review by PRC. The officials said that the competitive, dynamic, nature of the marketplace requires them to "go to market" quickly, which has to be balanced with the review process to ensure agreements generate profit for USPS.

USPS officials noted that the PRC review process for competitive product NSAs offers competitors the opportunity to undercut USPS's price. In 2011, PRC noted that "mailers have expressed concerns about the time and expense associated with NSAs" but concluded that "[e]xperience suggests that the time and effort required to put an NSA into effect is due, in greater part, to negotiating with the Postal Service and internal Postal Service review and approval rather than to the Commission's limited regulatory review."[22] Two mailers we spoke with also noted that they spent the majority of the time developing NSAs with USPS, not waiting for a PRC review. USPS officials noted that the time and effort that they spend on internal review and approval for international NSAs in particular are largely a result of the PRC's Rules of Practice. If the regulatory review were further streamlined, according to USPS, the time and effort needed to develop NSAs would be substantially reduced. PRC officials noted that as USPS and PRC have gained experience with competitive NSAs and streamlined the process, the average time has steadily decreased.

USPS has taken actions to streamline the process for developing competitive NSAs. First, to expedite and simplify the review of some competitive NSAs, USPS and PRC developed "umbrella" products. These products allow USPS to enter into NSAs that fall within a range of prices. A mailer may enter into such an NSA without pre-implementation review by PRC. According to USPS officials and PRC, this structure has facilitated the development of many NSAs, while maintaining an appropriate level of oversight. Second, USPS officials employ risk-based internal reviews, submitting NSAs with larger potential revenues to greater internal scrutiny than those with more limited potential before they

---

[22] PRC, *Section 701 Report.*

are provided to PRC for review. Finally, USPS has developed costing "templates" for its sales force. These templates include mail products' attributable costs, facilitating the sales forces' ability to offer discounts to mailers that allow USPS to at least cover its costs with the NSA.

To further streamline the process for developing NSAs, USPS has advocated for "after the fact" reviews of all competitive product NSAs. These reviews could improve NSAs' speed-to-market, as is currently done with the "umbrella" products discussed above. According to PRC officials, they have determined that it is best to allow after the fact reviews of certain types of NSAs only after USPS and PRC have gained experience with those types of NSAs and determined how to best improve data quality and collection.

Opportunities to Generate Net Revenue from Market Dominant NSAs Are Limited by Low Demand and Other Challenges

Price Increases for Market Dominant Products May Generate More Revenue than Discounts in NSAs

Opportunities to generate net revenue through market dominant product NSAs are limited. USPS's current estimates, as well as those of Christensen Associates on behalf of the USPS's OIG, suggest that First-Class Mail has low price elasticity.[23] These estimates mean that First-Class Mail volume is relatively insensitive to price changes and that recent volume declines are not related to the price of the postal products but to other factors, such as the lower cost of electronic communication. As a result, many mailers are not likely to respond to price decreases, such as discounts in NSAs, with additional mail volume, or to price increases with less volume. USPS's estimates also suggest that Standard Mail has relatively low price elasticity.

As a result of these price elasticities, price increases for some market dominant products may actually generate more revenue than discounts in market dominant NSAs. Indeed, it is likely that First-Class Mail as a whole

---

[23] USPS Office of Inspector General, White Paper, *Analysis of Postal Price Elasticities*, RARC-WP-13-008 (May 1, 2013).

could weather higher prices, according to the USPS OIG.[24] In theory, an attractive target for price increases would be products with low price elasticities, as modest price changes would likely have relatively minor effects on volume. As USPS commented in 2011, it might be rational, in some cases, to increase prices of profitable products with low elasticities.[25] First-Class Mail, and to a lesser extent Standard Mail, are highly profitable for USPS and have low price elasticities. There may therefore be additional revenue potential in the remaining First-Class Mail and Standard Mail volume, and capturing this intrinsic value by increasing prices is a common business practice. However, there may also be a point at which rate increases are self-defeating, potentially triggering large, permanent declines in mail volume. Also, market dominant products are subject to a price cap for each class of mail, limiting the extent to which USPS can increase the prices on, for example, First-Class Mail.

Data Limitations Create Challenges for Analyzing Market Dominant NSAs

USPS faces the difficulty of determining whether market dominant NSAs will increase volume and revenue. To show that market dominant NSAs improve the net financial position of USPS (i.e., create net revenue), PRC requires USPS to provide details about the expected improvements in USPS revenue resulting from any proposed NSA.[26] Estimating the net revenue generated by an NSA depends on accurately estimating how much mailers would mail in the absence of an agreement. Accordingly, PRC has directed that USPS provide it with details of projected mailer-specific costs, volumes, and revenues absent the NSA and as a result of the NSA.[27] To satisfy this requirement, USPS has generally used mail volume data, as well as expectations of future economic conditions, to develop projections of mailers' future volumes. However, USPS has not described to the PRC its precise methods for using past mail volume data and other qualitative factors used to develop these projections.

---

[24] USPS OIG, *Postal Service Revenue: Structure, Facts, and Future Possibilities.*

[25] PRC, *Section 701 Report* (USPS Response to Commission's Draft Section 701 Report).

[26] Market dominant NSAs must either improve the net financial position of USPS or enhance the performance of mail operations. 39 U.S.C. § 3622(c)(10)(A).

[27] PRC, *Order Establishing Ratemaking Regulations for Market Dominant and Competitive Products.*

While PRC has noted that "it is incumbent upon the Postal Service to develop a quantitative approach that incorporates the factors it is using to estimate volumes," this approach can be challenging because of data limitations.[28] One possible quantitative approach, suggested by PRC, to estimate mailer-specific volumes both in the absence of and as a result of an NSA is an elasticity model, using mailer-specific elasticities (that is, a measure of the mailer's sensitivity to price for a specific product). Using mailer-specific elasticities would allow for a precise estimation of volumes in the absence and as a result of an NSA. However, developing mailer-specific elasticities can be very difficult. According to PRC officials, estimation of mailer-specific price elasticities depends on having many observations of a mailer's volumes at different prices, in order to use statistical models to isolate the effect of price from all other factors that influence a mailer's volume. PRC has reported that when it is not possible to develop a mailer-specific elasticity, "the system-wide average for products will generally provide useable proxies."[29] However, as USPS has noted, the use of average product elasticities to estimate the results of NSAs, rather than mailer-specific elasticities, can be problematic, particularly when the response of individual mailers to NSAs are very different than the average response.[30] Further, according to a mailer we spoke with, USPS has little choice but to evaluate the projected net value of an NSA based on historical mail volumes and qualitative factors. The mailer explained that the projection of future mail volumes is inherently uncertain; even the mailer did not know how much it was going to mail in the next year.

---

[28] PRC, *Order Adding Discover Financial Services 1 Negotiated Service Agreement to the Market Dominant Product List*, Order No. 694, Docket No. MC2011-19, March 15, 2011.

[29] PRC, *Rate and Service Changes to Implement Functionally Equivalent Negotiated Service Agreement with Bank One Corporation, Opinion and Further Recommended Decision*, April 21, 2006.

[30] In its fiscal year 2012 *Annual Compliance Determination Report*, PRC also acknowledged "that the elasticity of individual mailers may differ from that of the class as a whole." They used average product elasticities, though, "because they are the only available elasticity estimates at this time." However, PRC officials also told us that the USPS model for estimating products' elasticities has not been updated to reflect new products and that such an update would likely have an impact on the accuracy and reliability of USPS's forecasts and NSA evaluations.

In a 2010 proceeding, PRC "sought suggestions from interested persons for new methods to estimate volume changes resulting from pricing-incentive programs of the Postal Service."[31] After comments from stakeholders, PRC concluded that "it is not persuaded that the alternatives offer a demonstrable improvement over the current method."[32] PRC encouraged USPS to identify a more reliable method for evaluating the impact of NSAs, sales, and promotions and to continue collecting data that could be used for that purpose. PRC said that the accuracy of analysis could be improved by USPS's willingness to collect mailer-specific, or even industry-specific, information. The lack of this data has frustrated PRC efforts to evaluate their financial impact. Ultimately, though, the case for pursuing NSAs must be a matter of business judgment by USPS management, according to USPS.

Although these data limitations may increase the risk that market dominant NSAs will lose money for USPS, they are partially mitigated by provisions in recent NSAs. USPS has implemented early-out clauses in NSAs to mitigate the risk posed by unclear projections of net revenue. For instance, the recent Discover NSA may be canceled at the end of any contract year, by either party, should the experience prove to be at odds with the parties' expectations. Further, when approving the Discover NSA, PRC estimated that the NSA was unlikely to improve USPS's net financial position but stated that "allowing this negotiated service agreement to proceed will allow management to enhance its knowledge of potential tools to slow the overall declining trend for First-Class Mail volume."[33] However, in the 2012 *Annual Compliance Determination Report*, PRC recommended that USPS re-evaluate the benefits and costs of continuing the NSA if it is not realizing a net benefit. As of May 2013, USPS had not canceled the contract.

---

[31] PRC, *Notice of Proposed Rulemaking Concerning Methods to Estimate Volume Changes Caused by Pricing Incentive Programs*, Order No. 469, Docket No. RM2010-9, June 8, 2010.

[32] PRC, *Order Terminating Proceeding*, Order No. 738, Docket No. RM2010-9, May 27, 2011.

[33] PRC, *Order Adding Discover Financial Services 1 Negotiated Service Agreement to the Market Dominant Product List.*

Mailers View the Process for Developing Market Dominant NSAs as Burdensome

Another challenge to generating additional revenue from market dominant product NSAs is that the process for developing these agreements can hinder the development of new agreements. Market dominant product NSAs are reviewed by PRC as part of a public proceeding. According to four mailers we spoke with, the fact that such NSAs go through a public process is a disincentive to developing such agreements. These mailers are sensitive about allowing any company-specific information to become public through the PRC review process. According to a 2011 USPS OIG report, transparency requirements, although prudent, make operating in a competitive marketplace difficult.[34] PRC officials told us, though, that the transparency of these proceedings helps balance the increased pricing flexibility granted to USPS under PAEA with the need for USPS accountability. Further, PRC regulations allow USPS to file confidential or proprietary information under seal, so that it remains nonpublic.[35]

Beyond the transparency concerns, many mailers are concerned about the time and resources needed to obtain a market dominant NSA. Many mailers we spoke with expressed concern about the length of time it took to develop NSAs. Officials from Valassis told us that they spent about 2 years negotiating its recent market dominant NSA, and officials for Discover said their negotiation lasted about a year. According to another mailer we spoke with, such long negotiations can hinder the ability to agree on an NSA because during these time periods the marketplace can shift, changing the incentives for mailers. PRC review times for these NSAs can also be substantial, though this time has decreased. For domestic, market dominant NSAs approved since the enactment of PAEA, the average review time was 88 days, whereas the average review time for those NSAs prior to PAEA was 214 days.

A major reason for the substantial time and resources needed to develop market dominant NSAs is that many such agreements have faced substantial opposition from mailers and stakeholders. In particular, some mailers and mailer industry associations have claimed that some proposed market dominant NSAs would harm the marketplace. By statute, market dominant NSAs "may not cause unreasonable harm to the marketplace."[36] In the proceeding for the most recent such NSA, with

---

[34] USPS OIG, *Postal Service Revenue: Structure, Facts, and Future Possibilities.*

[35] 39 CFR § 3007.10. Also see PRC, *Dockets Protected Materials Procedures.*

[36] 39 U.S.C. § 3622(c)(10)(B).

Valassis, a majority of commenters opposed the agreement because they claimed it would create an unfair competitive advantage for Valassis and harm the marketplace. Commenters said that the agreement would prevent other direct mail companies from competing on a level playing field, since Valassis would have a discount on its mail as part of the agreement. Some commenters also expressed concern that the NSA could negatively affect local newspapers by replacing the Sunday or weekend newspaper's preprinted advertising package—a crucial source of income, according to newspapers—with stand-alone direct mail from Valassis. Despite such opposition, though, PRC has approved both market dominant NSAs proposed since enactment of PAEA.[37]

Opportunities for Generating Net Revenue from Sales and Promotions Are Limited by Mail Use Changes and Limited Analysis of Long-term Impact

Opportunities to generate substantial additional revenue through sales and promotions are limited because of changes in the use of mail. Sales and promotions have been used for the market dominant products First-Class Mail and Standard Mail. As noted above, though, estimates indicate that demand for these market dominant products is low, and the volume for these products continues to decline. Further, the small scale of sales and promotions—often with short time frames and relatively small discounts—limit their impact for large mailers, since they may be unlikely to change their mailing patterns in response to a relatively small incentive. Two mailers we spoke with maintained that USPS's sales and promotions are most effective for small and medium sized mailers.

USPS has noted that by encouraging additional mail volume and revenue, sales and promotions provide pricing flexibility to mailers and help assure adequate revenues for USPS. By statute, sales and promotions must "help achieve" several objectives, such as assuring adequate revenues, to maintain financial stability.[38] Additionally, the system for regulating rates must take into account several factors, such as the requirement that each class of mail bear the direct and indirect

---

[37] PRC ultimately approved the Valassis NSA, noting that the deal would not cause unreasonable harm to the marketplace since the prices under the NSA are compensatory (i.e., in excess of attributable costs) and thus not anti-competitive. See PRC, *Order Approving Addition of Valassis Direct Mail, Inc. Negotiated Service Agreement to the Market Dominant Product List*, Order No. 1448, Docket No. MC2012-14, August 23, 2012. This decision has been challenged and is being reviewed by the U.S. Court of Appeals for the District of Columbia Circuit.

[38] 39 U.S.C. § 3622(b)(5).

costs attributable to that class of mail. (See app. II for a list of all objectives and factors.)

In support of sales and promotions when filing for approval with PRC, USPS has provided estimates of the financial result during the program time period. A few of these estimates for recent promotions have projected USPS to lose money during the program period. For example, USPS estimated that its 2011 mobile barcode promotion would reduce revenue by as much as $4.63 million. USPS has maintained, though, that promotions in particular can have value after the program period ends, so evaluating the financial effect based solely on mailer performance during the program period does not accurately reflect the true value of these programs. Indeed, USPS has stated that the long-term goal of promotions is to enhance the value of the mail for mailers, thereby helping sustain mail volume. USPS continues to implement a variety of such promotions, with six new domestic promotions planned for calendar year 2013.

According to USPS, it continues to refine the methodologies used to measure the long-term financial effects of sales and promotions, including tracking mailer behavior and surveying customers, but further data collection and analysis can be difficult. For example, without knowledge of mailers' planned mail volumes, USPS cannot precisely measure volume that would have been sent by mailers absent the sale or promotion. Further, attempts to gather data to estimate mailers' planned mail volumes can be difficult, as with market dominant NSAs. Nevertheless, USPS monitors the performance of promotion participants after the promotion period, and benchmarks their performance (i.e., mail volume) against their past performance, expected performance, and non-program participant performance.

Although not required to when filing for approval, USPS has not provided details to PRC on the long-term goals, the information it plans to collect in support of those goals, and the analysis it plans to perform to assess whether the long-term financial results of promotions met the intended goals. As a result, PRC has not assessed USPS methodologies for evaluating the long-term financial results of promotions. As USPS has noted, its financial challenge leaves little margin for error. Providing detailed data collection and analysis plans to PRC before implementation of promotions would allow USPS to better justify how these incentives help assure adequate revenues. PRC's assessment of these plans, as part of its approval decisions for promotions, would also help ensure that USPS promotions have positive financial results.

Conclusions

To achieve financial sustainability, USPS has been working to generate additional revenue to cover its costs. NSAs, sales, and promotions may help achieve this goal. Since enactment of PAEA in late 2006, USPS has made significant progress in using its increased pricing flexibility and generated billions of dollars in revenue through domestic and international NSAs. It is very unlikely, though, that additional net revenue created by NSAs will offset the revenue declines in other product areas. Additionally, the benefits, including long-term financial results, of promotions are not well understood by PRC and other postal stakeholders because USPS does not provide detailed information on its data collection and analysis plans to PRC before implementation. As a result, PRC has not had an opportunity to evaluate USPS's long-term goals and analysis plans for promotions. Though it can be difficult to collect and analyze data on the impact of promotions, given USPS's dire financial situation, demonstrating how promotions may achieve positive long-term financial results can help USPS maximize the revenue generated by those postage rate discounts.

Recommendations

Because USPS faces a deteriorating financial situation, we recommend that the following two actions be taken to help ensure that future promotions generate net revenue for USPS:

The Postmaster General should direct staff to provide specific data-collection methods and analytical processes for estimating the net financial results of promotions to PRC as part of USPS's request for PRC approval of all promotions.

The Chairman of the PRC should direct staff to evaluate USPS's data-collection and analysis plans for USPS's proposed mail promotions and discuss these evaluations in the PRC decisions for those mail promotions.

Agency Comments and Our Evaluation

We provided a draft of this report to USPS and PRC for review and comment. USPS and PRC both provided written comments in response, which are summarized below and included in their entirety in appendixes III and IV, respectively. In USPS's written response, USPS disagreed with the first recommendation and noted concerns regarding the characterizations of promotions, sales, and NSAs in the report. In separate correspondence, USPS also provided technical comments, which we incorporated as appropriate. In PRC's written response, PRC agreed with both recommendations and provided comments on NSAs.

Promotions

USPS stated that it disagreed with the first recommendation that USPS should provide specific data-collection methods and analytical processes for estimating the net financial results of promotions to PRC as part of USPS's request for PRC approval of all promotions. USPS stated that it does not believe the recommendation will significantly affect the PRC's review process, improve the quality of USPS's business decisions, or assure that promotions yield positive financial results. USPS noted that PRC has concluded that past promotions proposed by USPS comply with the relevant requirements, which emphasize the importance of pricing flexibility. PRC stated that it agreed with both recommendations and that it welcomes the opportunity to evaluate USPS's data-collection and analysis efforts for promotions.

We continue to believe that providing additional information to PRC on the potential long-term results would allow USPS to better justify promotions, and provide PRC with valuable additional information for its evaluation. Promotions for market dominant products must comply with several statutory objectives and factors, including that they help assure adequate revenues. When filing for approval, USPS has provided information to PRC estimating that some promotions may lose money during the program period. However, as USPS has noted, promotions are designed to increase the long-term value of mail, thereby helping to sustain mail volume and revenue. Given its dire financial situation, USPS should be commended for using its pricing flexibility to try and enhance its revenue. However, USPS has not provided information to PRC demonstrating how promotions could achieve these long-term goals. Providing information about the potential long-term financial results of promotions could help PRC better evaluate whether the proposed promotions help assure adequate revenues and comply with the other objectives and factors. USPS cannot afford to implement promotions without demonstrating how they can achieve positive long-term results.

USPS also stated in its letter that the report does not articulate how USPS could improve upon the methodologies it is using to conduct evaluations of promotions. We agree. We did not intend for the report to proscribe the methodologies that USPS should use to evaluate these long-term effects. Rather, the report concludes, though, that USPS's methodologies should be made available for PRC's evaluation prior to the implementation of promotions. This review would allow PRC to better evaluate the extent to which the promotions satisfy requirements.

USPS also provided additional comments related to promotions:

- In USPS's letter, USPS stated that the draft report concluded that promotions should not be offered unless USPS had "assurance" that promotions will achieve positive financial results. USPS correctly notes that no business decision is ever accompanied by a guarantee of success, and we have revised the relevant statement in our conclusions. However, as USPS agreed, sound analysis should accompany every business decision, including the implementation of promotions, particularly given USPS's financial situation.

- In its letter and technical comments, USPS stated that the report should more clearly delineate the differences between promotions and sales. In particular, USPS noted that promotions are designed to help sustain mail volume and revenue over the long-term. Sales, though, are designed to generate additional mail volumes, but only during the sale period itself. We have revised the relevant text throughout this report to better distinguish between the different goals of sales and promotions.

- In USPS's letter, USPS also notes that some of the costs for recent promotions have been recovered through the creation of additional price cap authority, mitigating the risk of financial losses from the most recent promotions. USPS is to be commended for seeking ways to mitigate the financial risks of any postage rate discount, as it has done with early-out clauses in market dominant NSAs. However, in a recent decision approving a promotion, PRC did not accept the price cap treatment proposed by USPS.[39]

- In its letter, USPS also requested that we characterize the data provided by USPS to PRC on some sales not as "corrupt" but "incomplete" or "insufficient." The term "corrupt" is not meant to imply that USPS intended to make data provided to PRC unusable. However, according to PRC, data provided to it by USPS on an early

---

[39] PRC, *Order Approving Technology Credit Promotion*, Order No. 1743, Docket No. R2013-6, June 10, 2013. USPS sought to recover revenue equal to the rebates from the promotion by creating new pricing authority that it could use at the time of the next annual price adjustment. This issue is also under broader review by PRC (see PRC Docket No. RM2013-2). Several parties have advised PRC to bar USPS from recovering as rate adjustment authority any revenue that is forgone because of promotions.

sale was "corrupt" and hindered PRC's ability to evaluate the financial results of that effort. We did not modify the report related to this issue.

NSAs

USPS also disagreed with the statement in the report that many mailers are not likely to respond to price decreases, such as discounts in market dominant NSAs, with additional mail volume. USPS stated that market dominant NSAs can provide promising opportunities to increase mail volumes and revenues in the future. Our conclusion about market dominant NSAs is based primarily on USPS's estimates indicating that market dominant mail products have low elasticities. These estimates are a measure of the degree to which mailers respond to price changes and alter their demand for products and services. However, these estimates are product-wide averages. To the extent individual mailers have elasticities different from the average, it may be possible to incentivize additional mail volume from those mailers through price decreases. Few mailers, though, are likely to have an elasticity different enough from the average to warrant such an agreement.

PRC also clarified two points in the report related to market dominant NSAs. First, PRC noted that USPS's methodologies for assessing the financial impact of market dominant NSAs are not considered authoritative under statutory and regulatory requirements unless and until such methodologies are accepted by PRC as "accepted analytical principles" under sections 3050.10 and 3050.1(a) of the Code of Federal Regulations, Title 39. Second, PRC noted that after-the-fact review of NSAs works well for Non-Published Rate contracts, but is not applicable for agreements not subject to established, specific limitations that assure consistency with applicable statutory requirements. No change to the report was necessary based on these comments.

As we agreed with your office, unless you publicly announce the contents of this report earlier, we plan no further distribution of it until 30 days from the date of this letter. At that time, we will send copies of this report to the appropriate congressional committees, Postmaster General, Chairman of PRC, USPS OIG, and other interested parties. In addition, the report will be available at no charge on GAO's website at http://www.gao.gov.

If you or your staff have any questions regarding this report, please contact me at (202) 512-2834 or stjamesl@gao.gov. Contact points for our Offices of Congressional Relations and Public Affairs may be found on the last page of this report. GAO staff who made key contributions to this report are listed in appendix V.

Lorelei St. James
Director
Physical Infrastructure Issues

Appendix I: Scope and Methodology

To describe the NSAs, sales and promotions U.S. Postal Service (USPS) has developed, as well as their reported financial results, we reviewed public and non-public documents as well as additional USPS data. To summarize the financial results of NSAs, we examined non-public versions of USPS's Cost and Revenue Analysis reports for fiscal years 2009 through 2012. We also reviewed non-public documents that included the volume, cost, and revenue of active competitive, domestic NSAs, for fiscal years 2009 through 2012. There were no active domestic competitive NSAs in fiscal years 2007 and 2008. We also reviewed non-public documents that included the volume, cost, and revenue of active competitive, international NSAs, for fiscal years 2007 through 2012. We also reviewed the data collection reports for market dominant NSAs. To confirm our summaries of the number and results of NSAs, we also obtained additional data from USPS on the number of active NSAs, by fiscal year, as well as the estimated financial results of all market dominant NSAs. We also reviewed Postal Regulatory Commission's (PRC) *Annual Compliance Determination Report* for fiscal years 2007 through 2012, to identify, where applicable, which competitive NSAs PRC determined covered their attributable costs. We also reviewed PRC's conclusions in these reports about the financial results of market dominant NSAs. To summarize the number of, and results from, USPS sales and promotions to date, we reviewed USPS documents filed with PRC requesting approval for sales and promotions as well as PRC's *Annual Compliance Determination Reports*. We also obtained additional data from USPS on the estimated results of sales and promotions.

To put the financial results of incentives into context of USPS's overall financial situation, we also examined other USPS documents. These included the Revenue, Pieces, and Weights reports for fiscal years 2007 through 2012 and the fiscal year 2012 Form 10-K filing.[1] Further, we also obtained USPS projections of future mail revenue and volume.

We assessed the reliability of these data sources by interviewing USPS officials. Based on this information, we determined that the data provided to us were sufficiently reliable for our reporting purposes.

---

[1] The Form 10-K report is also called the Annual Report Pursuant to Section 13 or 15(d) of the Securities Exchange Act of 1934.

We also conducted interviews with USPS and PRC officials, as well as 15 mailers that have participated in NSAs, sales, and promotions, on the financial condition of USPS and the results of those incentives, in order to enhance our understanding of the circumstances in which these incentives are developed and implemented. In these interviews we also discussed potential limitations to USPS and PRC analyses of incentives' results. See below for information on how we selected mailers to interview.

To identify and assess any opportunities to generate additional revenue from NSAs, sales, and promotions, as well as challenges, if any, that could the hinder their development and implementation, we conducted interviews with a variety of stakeholders. We conducted interviews with officials from USPS, PRC, and 15 mailers that both have and have not participated in USPS incentives (see list below). In order to obtain a range of perspectives on the opportunities and challenges related to NSAs, sales, and promotions, we identified mailers that have participated in NSAs involving a variety of competitive and market dominant products, and both international and domestic mail. We also identified mailers that had not participated in NSAs. Among these mailers, we interviewed both large and small mailers, defined as whether the mailer had more or less than $250 million in annual revenue in the most recent fiscal year for which data or estimates were available, as well as some that were recommended to us by a mailer association. Finally, we interviewed industry associations that represent major mailers in order to gather additional perspectives on the opportunities and challenges associated with NSAs, sales, and promotions, including the Association for Postal Commerce, Direct Marketing Association, National Newspaper Association, and Newspaper Association of America. The views of mailers and industry associations cannot be generalized to all mailers and industry associations because they were selected as part of a nonprobability sample.

Mailers Interviewed

- 4imprint
- Amazon
- AT&T
- Barnes & Noble
- Canada Post
- Discover Financial Services
- FedEx SmartPost
- Gardens Alive!

- Harriet Carter Gifts
- Highlights for Children, Inc.
- Pitney Bowes
- Quad/Graphics
- UPS
- Valassis
- Valpak

To further identify and assess opportunities and challenges related to NSAs, sales, and promotions, we also reviewed a variety of documents. First, we reviewed the 2007 PRC regulations governing NSAs. Second, we reviewed a variety of PRC proceedings, including its 2010 proceeding to investigate methodologies for estimating volume changes due to pricing incentive programs, and its recommended decisions for all domestic, market dominant NSAs approved to date. We also examined PRC approval decisions for other NSAs in order to document the length of the PRC review process. We also reviewed the internal business evaluations conducted by USPS for a variety of domestic, competitive NSAs. Finally, we reviewed findings from relevant USPS Office of Inspector General reports. We determined that the methodologies of these reports were sufficiently reliable for our purposes.

Appendix II: Required Objectives and Factors for Sales and Promotions

As part of the review for a proposed sale or promotion or market dominant products, PRC evaluates whether the sale or promotion satisfies the requirements of postal rate regulation.[1] As listed below, these requirements include several objectives that the sale or promotion must be designed to achieve and several factors that PRC must take into account.

Objectives

(1) To maximize incentives to reduce costs and increase efficiency.

(2) To create predictability and stability in rates.

(3) To maintain high quality service standards established under section 3691.

(4) To allow the Postal Service pricing flexibility.

(5) To assure adequate revenues, including retained earnings, to maintain financial stability.

(6) To reduce the administrative burden and increase the transparency of the ratemaking process.

(7) To enhance mail security and deter terrorism.

(8) To establish and maintain a just and reasonable schedule for rates and classifications, however the objective under this paragraph shall not be construed to prohibit the Postal Service from making changes of unequal magnitude within, between, or among classes of mail.

(9) To allocate the total institutional costs of the Postal Service appropriately between market-dominant and competitive products.

Factors

(1) the value of the mail service actually provided each class or type of mail service to both the sender and the recipient, including but not limited to the collection, mode of transportation, and priority of delivery;

---

[1] See 39 U.S.C. § 3622.

(2) the requirement that each class of mail or type of mail service bear the direct and indirect postal costs attributable to each class or type of mail service through reliably identified causal relationships plus that portion of all other costs of the Postal Service reasonably assignable to such class or type;

(3) the effect of rate increases upon the general public, business mail users, and enterprises in the private sector of the economy engaged in the delivery of mail matter other than letters;

(4) the available alternative means of sending and receiving letters and other mail matter at reasonable costs;

(5) the degree of preparation of mail for delivery into the postal system performed by the mailer and its effect upon reducing costs to the Postal Service;

(6) simplicity of structure for the entire schedule and simple, identifiable relationships between the rates or fees charged the various classes of mail for postal services;

(7) the importance of pricing flexibility to encourage increased mail volume and operational efficiency;

(8) the relative value to the people of the kinds of mail matter entered into the postal system and the desirability and justification for special classifications and services of mail;

(9) the importance of providing classifications with extremely high degrees of reliability and speed of delivery and of providing those that do not require high degrees of reliability and speed of delivery;

(10) the desirability of special classifications for both postal users and the Postal Service in accordance with the policies of this title, including agreements between the Postal Service and postal users, when available on public and reasonable terms to similarly situated mailers, that—

(A) either—

(i) improve the net financial position of the Postal Service through reducing Postal Service costs or increasing the overall contribution to the institutional costs of the Postal Service; or

(ii) enhance the performance of mail preparation, processing, transportation, or other functions; and

(B) do not cause unreasonable harm to the marketplace.

(11) the educational, cultural, scientific, and informational value to the recipient of mail matter;

(12) the need for the Postal Service to increase its efficiency and reduce its costs, including infrastructure costs, to help maintain high quality, affordable postal services;

(13) the value to the Postal Service and postal users of promoting intelligent mail and of secure, sender-identified mail; and

(14) the policies of this title as well as such other factors as the Commission determines appropriate.

Appendix III: Comments from the United States Postal Service

Nahsca M. Manse
Chief Marketing and Sales Officer
Executive Vice President

UNITED STATES
POSTAL SERVICE

June 7, 2013

Ms. Lorelei St. James
Director, Physical Infrastructure
United States Government Accountability Office
Washington, DC 20548-0001

Dear Ms. St. James:

Thank you for providing the United States Postal Service (USPS) with the opportunity to review and comment on the draft report titled *U.S. Postal Service: Opportunities to Increase Revenue Exist with Competitive Products; Additional Reviews Could Better Inform Promotion Decisions* (GAO-13-578). To assist with the Government Accountability Office's (GAO) review of USPS's comments, this letter is divided into three sections. In the first section, USPS addresses its general concerns with the GAO's recommendation. In the second section, USPS addresses specific concerns regarding the GAO's discussion of Negotiated Service Agreements (NSA). In the third section, USPS addresses specific concerns regarding the GAO's characterization of promotions and sales.

<u>General</u>:

While the USPS is committed to providing the Postal Regulatory Commission (PRC) with any information or evidence it requests, it respectfully disagrees with the GAO's recommendation. In particular, the USPS does not believe that the GAO's recommendation to the Postmaster General will significantly impact the PRC's review process, improve the quality of the United States Postal Service's business decisions, or assure that promotions yield positive financial results.

First, as the GAO is undoubtedly aware, the regulatory review process for promotions is not aimed at concluding whether a promotion will in fact succeed in the long run. Rather, as provided by 39 U.S.C. § 3622, the PRC has the obligation to determine whether each promotion complies with statutory policies, including 21 objectives and factors, which emphasize, *inter alia*, efficiency, service levels, and pricing flexibility. Based on these standards, the PRC has repeatedly concluded (without the additional information recommended by the GAO) that the USPS promotions provide pricing flexibility, represent important long-term strategies, and comply with the standards outlined in Title 39. *See, e.g.*, PRC Order No 1296, at 7-9 (Mar. 26, 2012), PRC Order No. 1424, at 7-10 (Aug. 7, 2012).

Additionally, the USPS disagrees with the GAO's conclusion that promotions should not be offered unless it has "assurance" that the promotions will achieve positive financial results. GAO Report, at 26. While the USPS agrees that sound analysis should accompany every business decision, it respectfully contends that no business decision is ever accompanied by a guarantee of success. Indeed, every business decision (including those aimed at reducing costs) poses risks that management must do its best to account for and overcome. If the USPS is to remain a viable entity well into the future, it must, despite its current financial constraints, continue

to make strategic and innovative investments in its future. While every investment may not succeed as originally planned, postal management remains confident that the promotions are

475 L'Enfant Plaza SW
Washington DC 20260-5002
www.usps.com

to make strategic and innovative investments in its future. While every investment may not succeed as originally planned, postal management remains confident that the promotions are having their intended long-term effect of sustaining mail volumes by increasing the value of advertising mail.

NSA's:

With respect to Market-Dominant NSAs, the GAO states that due to the "low price elasticities" of First-Class Mail and Standard Mail "mailers are not likely to respond to price decreases, such as discounts in NSAs with additional mail volume." GAO Report, at 20. In this regard, USPS has argued during the review of past Market-Dominant NSA's that there are a variety of other factors (e.g. a customer's marketing strategy) and market conditions (e.g. competition amongst mailers) that can encourage a customer to generate new mail volume. Such factors militate in favor of the USPS entering into individual business arrangements with specific customers. Accordingly, the USPS continues to believe that the Market-Dominant NSAs can provide promising opportunities to increase mail volumes and revenues in the future.

Promotions:

With respect to promotions, the USPS would encourage the GAO to more clearly delineate the differences between promotions and sales throughout its report. As the GAO has accurately articulated in several locations, promotions are designed to generate additional mail volumes in the future by increasing the long-term value of mail. Promotions accomplish this goal by using postage discounts to encourage mailers to integrate technology (e.g. mobile barcodes) with physical mail pieces. In contrast, sales offer temporary postage discounts that are only designed to generate additional mail volumes during the sale period itself. The USPS feels that it is important to make this distinction throughout the report, since its institutional focus has recently shifted to promotions.

Additionally, the GAO concludes that "the benefits, including long-term financial results of promotions are not well understood because USPS does not provide detailed information on its data collection and analysis plans to the PRC before implementation." GAO Report, at 26. While the USPS agrees that it must monitor and track the long-term effects of promotions on mailer behavior, the GAO has not articulated how the USPS could improve upon the methodologies it is already using to conduct such evaluations. The GAO itself recognizes that "attempts to gather data to estimate mailers' planned mail volumes can be difficult." GAO Report, at 25. Without more specific recommendations for improvement, the USPS is concerned that the GAO's recommendation unnecessarily creates the appearance that promotions are somehow risky and should only be pursued if there are assurances of success.

Such an appearance is unjustified given that nearly every USPS analysis, along with Table 4 of the report, indicates that promotions have had a net-positive financial effect during the promotion periods. The USPS believes that this net-positive financial result will only increase when the promotion's long-term impact on mailer behavior is evaluated. As the GAO notes, the USPS monitors these long-term effects by continuously tracking mailer behavior and by conducting surveys after each promotion. Through this monitoring, and through informal discussions with mailers, USPS has repeatedly learned about the positive impacts the promotions have already had on customers' behavior. Such positive impacts include:

- Accelerating customer adoption of certain technologies;
- Increasing selected customers' overall mail volumes; and
- Elevating the status of mail (within our customers' marketing groups) as an essential tool for developing successful multi-channel marketing campaigns.

Survey results supporting these findings, along with several customer testimonials, are included as Attachment A.

Further, setting aside whether promotions generate additional volumes themselves, the GAO should consider the fact that some of the costs for recent promotions have been recovered through the creation of additional price cap authority. For example, in compliance with PRC rules, USPS successfully recovered a large portion of the forgone revenue from its FY 2013 promotions through offsetting rate increases. Accordingly, regardless of the promotion's ability to immediately or prospectively generate additional mail volumes/revenues, USPS has taken steps to mitigate the risk of financial losses from its most recent promotions.

With respect to sales, the GAO states that according to the PRC "they have not evaluated the results of all sales because of corrupt or missing USPS data." GAO Report at 14. The USPS is concerned that the use of the term corrupt implies that it intended to make data provided to the PRC unusable. Though the USPS admits that some of the data it has provided may have been imperfect, such imperfections were never intended and were always corrected when brought to the USPS' attention. The USPS would encourage the GAO to replace the word corrupt with "incomplete" or "insufficient." Such words would not only be more accurate, but would also be consistent with the GAO's treatment of similar data issues throughout the report.

In short, the USPS would encourage the GAO to do three things with respect to its discussion of promotions and sales: 1) clearly acknowledge the steps that the USPS has taken to ensure the success of each promotion and prevent financial losses; 2) clearly delineate promotions from sales; and 3) replace the word "corrupt" with "insufficient" or "incomplete" when describing data provided to the PRC concerning sales. The USPS hopes that these modifications will ensure that promotions are not needlessly cast in a negative light due to the GAO's own belief that the USPS should be doing more to analyze the long-term impacts of these programs.

Again, the United States Postal Service thanks the GAO for the opportunity to comment on its draft report. If you or your staff wish to discuss any of these comments further, I am available at your convenience.

Sincerely,

Nagisa Manabe

Attachment

Attachment A

<u>Mobile Commerce and Personalization (MCPP) and Holiday Mobile Shopping (HMSP)
Promotions - Survey Insights and Customer Testimonials:</u>

- A sizable percentage of mailers initiated changes to their digital strategy as a result of
the promotions.

  - Approximately 30 percent of MCPP survey respondents and 25 percent of HMSP
    survey respondents made changes to their website in order to meet the requirements
    for participation in the promotion.

  Omaha Steaks:
  *"Encouraged by the postal incentive, (We) tested the inclusion of a QR (quick response) code
  on mailings as an easy way for customers to order through the website. Because of the
  response, the QR code has now rolled out in most of (our) mailings."*

- There was an impact on mail volume as a result of the promotions.

  - About 20 percent of MCPP survey respondents increased the number of pieces
    mailed because of the promotion. Additionally, approximately 46 percent of
    respondents indicated that they would use the 2 percent savings from this promotion
    to send more direct mail and/or to increase the page count of mailings.
  - Approximately, 14 percent of HMSP respondents indicated they had increased
    mailing volume because of the promotion. Additionally, 48 percent indicated they
    would reinvest the savings from the price discount to send more direct mail and/or to
    increase the page count of mailings.

  Amerimark/Dr.Leonard's:
  *"Mail definitely does not "just happen." In fact, it is quite the opposite. Postage costs (for
  catalog mailing and package shipment) are the second largest expense of our business and
  our business model is extremely sensitive to decisions made by the U.S. Postal Service, as
  well as opportunities created by the USPS."*

  *"When promotions are offered, we analyze the financial impact and often increase the
  quantities of our catalog mailings to test the idea/promotion, but just as importantly prospect
  for new customers and grow our business, resulting in higher levels of future postage
  (catalogs and packages)."*

  IBIS World:
  *"During the year, operators will benefit from programs implemented by the U.S. Postal
  Service to encourage commercial mailers. This factor is expected to contribute to revenue
  growth of 0.3 percent during 2013."*

- The promotions had a limited but measurable impact on improving perceptions of the
USPS brand.

  - Approximately 38 percent of MCPP survey respondents and 35 percent of HMSP
    survey respondents strongly agreed with the statement that they perceived the
    U.S. Postal Service as being more innovative than they did before as a result of
    the promotion.

Carol Klierwers':

"The USPS is our primary delivery carrier due to their ability to deliver our Standard Mail flats and letters, Parcel Select light weight packages, First-Class Mail and Priority Mail effectively. We've been fortunate enough to work with high caliber leaders, within their organization, that bring us solutions and recommendations that enable us to provide our clients the best service in the industry today. With the support of our Strategic Account Manager, the Business Service Network and Business Mail Entry Unit Management, we enable our Logistics network to utilize the USPS resources to the benefit of our clients and customers and exceed their expectations. Over the past few years, the USPS has brought innovative ideas to our attention for deployment that help us stay current."

- Approximately four-fifths of HMSP survey respondents who used mobile barcodes in the past, representing about three-fourths of all participants in the promotion, could be fairly characterized as "entrenched users" of mobile barcodes by virtue of the fact they now have employed mobile barcodes on at least two mailings and say that they will continue to use them in the future.

Appendix IV: Comments from the Postal Regulatory Commission

UNITED STATES OF AMERICA
POSTAL REGULATORY COMMISSION

RUTH Y. GOLDWAY
CHAIRMAN

June 5, 2013

Ms. Lorelei St. James
Director, Physical Infrastructure
Government Accountability Office
441 G Street, NW
Washington, DC 20548

Dear Ms. St. James:

Thank you for the opportunity to offer comments on the Government Accountability Office's (GAO) draft report titled *U.S. Postal Service: Opportunities to Increase Revenue Exist with Competitive Products; Additional Reviews Could Better Inform Promotions Decisions* (GAO-13-578).

The GAO made two recommendations in this draft report:

(1)   As part of its requests for approval, the U.S. Postal Service (Postal Service) should provide the Commission with specific data collection methods and analytical processes for estimating the long-term net financial results of promotions.

(2)   As a follow up to the first recommendation, the Commission should evaluate the long-term Postal Service data collection and analysis plans for mail promotions provided to the Commission under the first recommendation.

The Commission agrees with both recommendations.

Prior to review of this draft report, the Commission was not aware that the Postal Service was collecting data on the effectiveness of promotions by tracking mailing behavior, surveying customers, and benchmarking promotion participants' performance against past performance, expected performance, and non-program participant performance. The Commission welcomes the opportunity to evaluate such data collection and analysis efforts.

The Commission found the report well-researched and balanced. However, there are two points that the Commission would like to clarify. First, the Postal Service's methodologies for assessing the financial impact of market dominant negotiated service agreements (NSAs) are not considered authoritative under statutory and regulatory requirements unless and until such methodologies are accepted by the Commission as "accepted analytical principles" under 39 CFR 3050.10 and 3050.1(a); *see also* 39 U.S.C. 3652 (requiring the Commission to prescribe "the content and form of the public reports...to be provided by the Postal Service.").

901 NEW YORK AVENUE, NW • SUITE 200 WEST • WASHINGTON, DC 20268-0001

Ms. St. James
June 5, 2013
Page 2 of 2

As noted in the draft report, the Commission initiated a proceeding to consider updating the accepted methodology with respect to more accurately and reliably measuring both the expected and actual financial impacts of NSAs and other pricing incentives. In its comments in that proceeding, the Postal Service concluded that, while quantitative evaluation methods might help inform the decision making process, "ultimately, the case for pursuing incentive programs must be a matter of business judgment by Postal Service management." Recognizing its responsibility for basing decisions on more reliable and accountable grounds, the Commission terminated the proceeding and retained the prior accepted analytical principles regarding the measurement of the expected and actual financial impacts of NSAs and other pricing incentives. As with all accepted analytical principles, at any time interested parties, including the Postal Service, may request that the Commission review its approved methodology for assessing the impact of NSAs and other pricing incentives. See 39 CFR 3050.11.

Second, the draft report states that "[a]ccording to PRC officials, they have determined that it is best to allow after-the-fact reviews of certain types of NSAs only after USPS and PRC have gained experience with those types of NSAs and determined how to best improve data quality and collection." The Commission notes that this statement refers to agreements known as Non-Published Rates (NPR) contracts, which are based on a contract template that ensures compliance with all statutory and regulatory requirements. While this approach works well for the applications to which NPR contracts are best suited, it is not applicable for agreements not subject to established specific limitations that assure consistency with applicable statutory requirements.

Thank you for the opportunity to comment on this draft report. The Commission appreciates GAO's collaboration and careful efforts on this report. Consistent with its statutory responsibilities, the Commission remains committed to providing helpful and accurate reviews to better inform Postal Service revenue generation opportunities.

Sincerely,

Ruth Y. Goldway
Chairman

Appendix V: GAO Contact and Staff Acknowledgments

GAO Contact	Lorelei St. James, (202) 512-2834 or stjamesl@gao.gov.
Staff Acknowledgments	In addition to the contact named above, Teresa Anderson (Assistant Director), Ken Bombara, Kyle Browning, Colin Fallon, Imoni Hampton, Josh Ormond, Sara Ann Moessbauer, and Crystal Wesco made key contributions to this report.